PIANO · VOCAL · GUITAR

You Raise Me Up
SONGS OF INSPIRATION

Alfred

Produced by
Alfred Music Publishing Co., Inc.
P.O. Box 10003
Van Nuys, CA 91410-0003
alfred.com

Printed in USA.

No part of this book shall be reproduced, arranged, adapted, recorded, publicly performed, stored in a retrieval system, or transmitted by any means without written permission from the publisher. In order to comply with copyright laws, please apply for such written permission and/or license by contacting the publisher at alfred.com/permissions.

ISBN-10: 0-7390-7215-3
ISBN-13: 978-0-7390-7215-8

Cover Photo of leafy branch: © iStockphoto / Dole08

 Alfred Cares. Contents printed on 100% recycled paper.

Contents

Title	Page
Amazing Grace	4
Anyway	6
Believe in Yourself	12
Blessed	16
The Blessing	25
Bridge Over Troubled Water	30
A Change Is Gonna Come	38
Everything Is Beautiful	42
From a Distance	48
Greatest Love of All	63
Heal the World	56
Heart	53
Hero	68
(Your Love Keeps Lifting Me) Higher and Higher	74
I Believe	78
I Can See Clearly Now	82
In My Daughter's Eyes	86
It's in Every One of Us	100
Just a Closer Walk with Thee	98
Lift Every Voice and Sing	104

TITLE	PAGE
LIVE LIKE YOU WERE DYING	91
LOOK TO THE RAINBOW	124
MAN IN THE MIRROR	107
THE MORNING AFTER	120
OH HAPPY DAY	129
ONE MOMENT IN TIME	134
(THERE'LL BE) PEACE IN THE VALLEY	139
THE PRAYER	142
SHOWER THE PEOPLE	150
SOFTLY AND TENDERLY	154
TOUCH THE HEM OF HIS GARMENT	156
UP WHERE WE BELONG	166
WHAT A WONDERFUL WORLD	170
WHEN YOU BELIEVE	159
WHEN YOU'RE SMILING	174
WHO I WAS BORN TO BE	178
THE WIND BENEATH MY WINGS	184
YOU LIGHT UP MY LIFE	191
YOU RAISE ME UP	194
YOU'RE THE INSPIRATION	199

AMAZING GRACE

TRADITIONAL

© 2010 ALFRED MUSIC PUBLISHING CO., INC.
All Rights Reserved

ANYWAY

Words and Music by
MARTINA McBRIDE, BRAD WARREN
and BRETT WARREN

© 2006 DELEMMAVA MUSIC PUBLISHING, STYLESONIC MUSIC, LLC and BUCKY AND CLYDE MUSIC
All Rights on behalf of itself and BUCKY AND CLYDE MUSIC Administered by STYLESONIC MUSIC, LLC
All Rights Reserved

al-ways turn out like_ I think it should,_ but I do it an-y-way._

_ I do it an-y-way._

decresc.

Verse 2:

2. This world's_gone cra-zy, and it's hard to be-lieve_ that to-

mor-row will_ be bet-ter than_ to-day._ Be-lieve it

D.S. ℅ al Coda

BELIEVE IN YOURSELF

Words and Music by
CHARLIE SMALLS

Believe in Yourself - 4 - 1

© 1974 (Renewed) WARNER-TAMERLANE PUBLISHING CORP.
All Rights Reserved

14

BLESSED

Words and Music by
TROY VERGES, BRETT JAMES
and HILLARY LINDSEY

© 2001 FSMGI (IMRO), SONGS OF UNIVERSAL, INC. (BMI), SONY/ATV SONGS LLC (ASCAP),
ANIMAL FAIR (ASCAP) and SONY/ATV MUSIC PUBLISHING LLC (ASCAP)
All Rights for FSMGI (IMRO) Administered by STATE ONE MUSIC AMERICA (BMI)
All Rights Reserved

Verse 1:

kissed by the sun each morn-ing; put my feet on a hard-wood floor.___

I get to___ hear my chil-dren laugh - ing___ down the

hall through the bed-room door.___ Some-times I sit on my___ front porch___

___ swing, just soak-in' up the day.___ I think to my-self, I

To Coda ⊕

Verse 2:

Blessed - 9 - 4

Lyrics:

I have been blessed.____

Bridge:

When I, when I'm sing-in' my kids to sleep,____ when I feel you____

Chorus:

THE BLESSING

Words and Music by
DAVID DOWNES and BRENDAN GRAHAM

Largo, con rubato ♩ = c.50

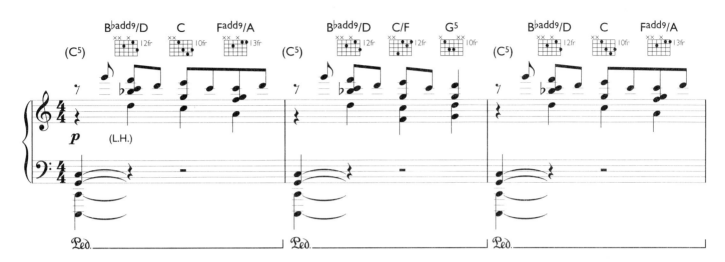

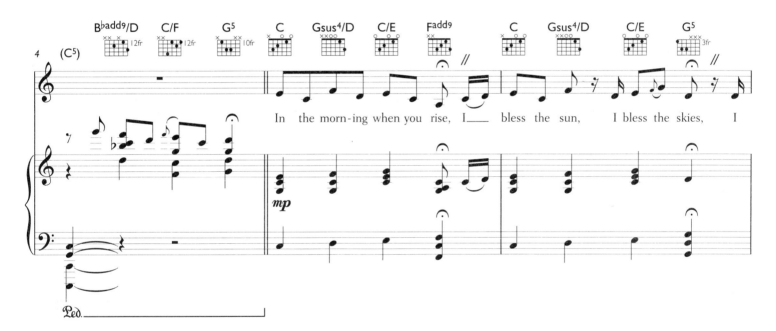

In the morn-ing when you rise, I___ bless the sun, I bless the skies, I

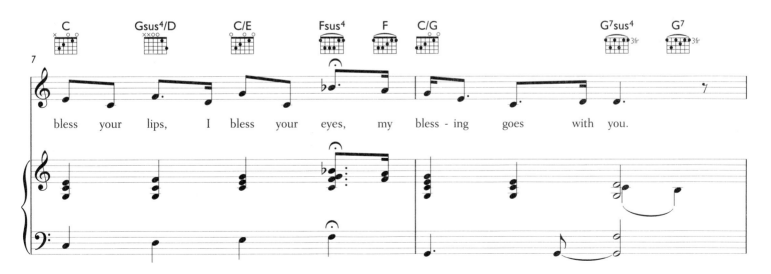

bless your lips, I bless your eyes, my bless-ing goes with you.

The Blessing - 5 - 1

© 2007 LIFFEY PUBLISHING LTD, Dublin 2, Ireland and PEERMUSIC (UK) LTD, London WC1X 8LZ
All Rights Reserved

When the storms of life are strong, when you're wound-ed, when you don't be-long, when

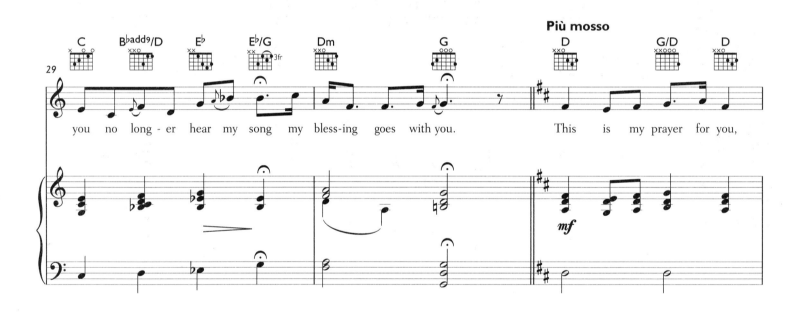

you no long-er hear my song my bless-ing goes with you. This is my prayer for you,

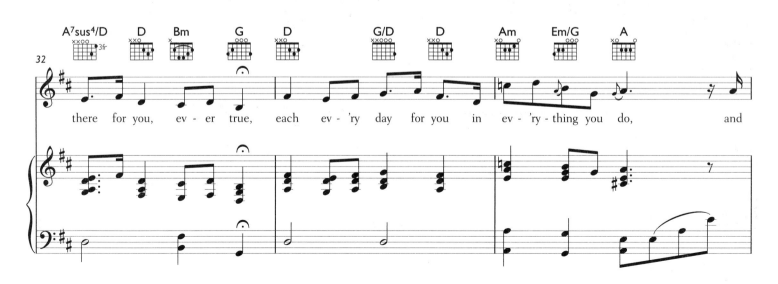

there for you, ev-er true, each ev-'ry day for you in ev-'ry-thing you do, and

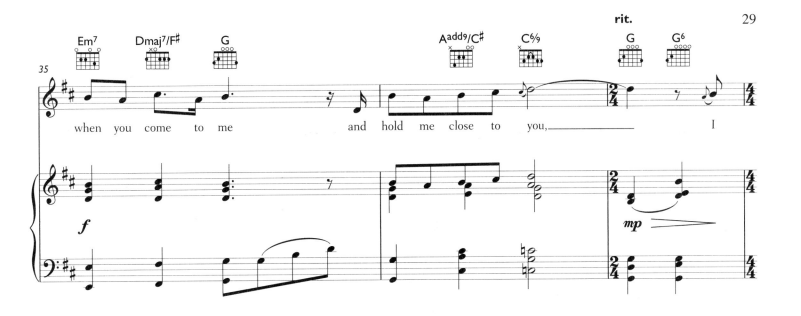

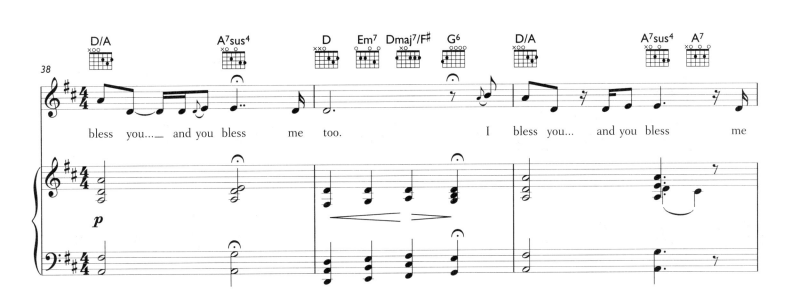

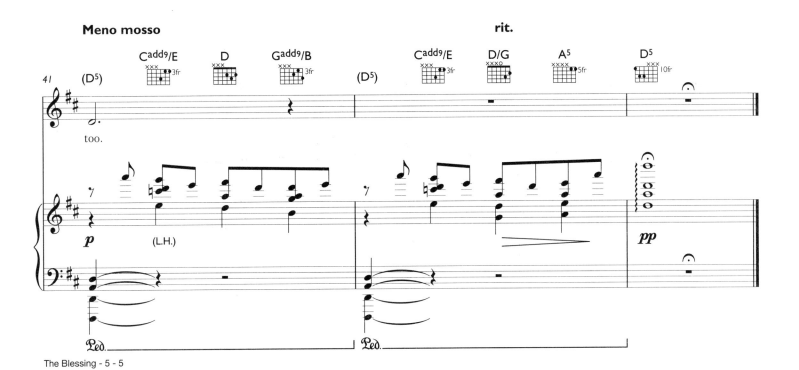

BRIDGE OVER TROUBLED WATER

Words and Music by
PAUL SIMON

Moderately slow ♩ = 84

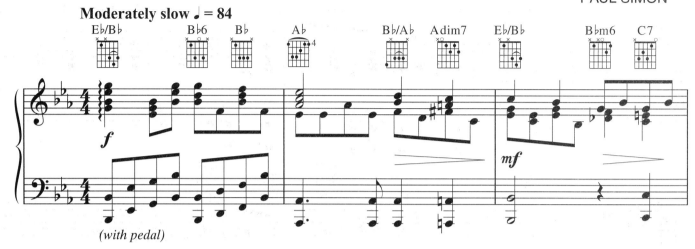

(with pedal)

Verse 1:

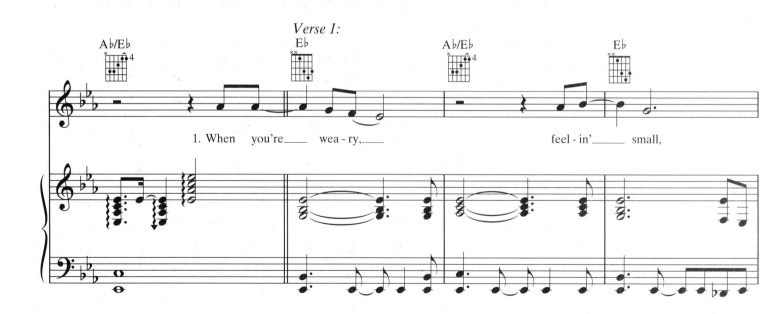

1. When you're____ wea - ry,____ feel - in'____ small,

© 1969 (Renewed) PAUL SIMON (BMI)
Used by Permission of MUSIC SALES CORPORATION
All Rights Reserved

A CHANGE IS GONNA COME

Words and Music by
SAM COOKE

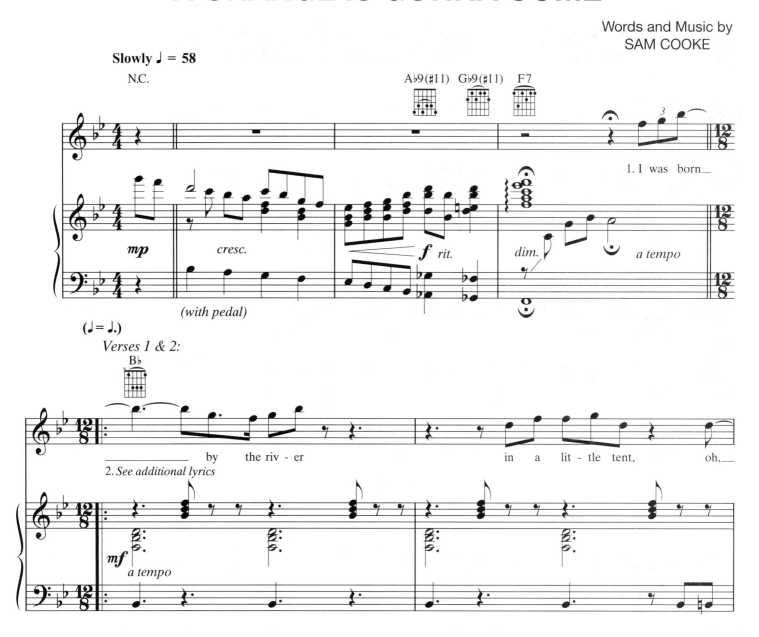

A Change Is Gonna Come - 4 - 1

© 1964 (Renewed) ABKCO MUSIC, INC., 85 Fifth Avenue, New York, NY 10003
All Rights Reserved

Gm

hang a-round.___ It's been a long,_____ a long

Bb

To Coda ⊕

Cm7   Eb7   D7   Gm

time com-ing,_____ but I know,___ oh-oo-oh,___ a change gon' come,___ oh

Bb   Cm7

Bridge:

yes, it will.   Then I go, oh-oo-oh,_____ to my___

Bb6   Cm7

___ broth-er___   and I say, broth-er,___ help me___

Verse 2:
It's been too hard living but I'm afraid to die
'Cause I don't know what's up there beyond the sky.
It's been a long, a long time comin',
But I know, oh-oo-oh,
A change gonna come, oh yes, it will.

Verse 4:
There've been times that I thought
I couldn't last for long
But now I think I'm able to carry on
It's been a long, a long time comin',
but I know, oh-oo-oh, a change gonna come, oh yes, it will.

EVERYTHING IS BEAUTIFUL

Words and Music by
RAY STEVENS

© 1970 (Renewed) AHAB MUSIC COMPANY, INC.
All Rights Reserved   Used by Permission

Verse 2:
We shouldn't care about the length of his hair or the color of his skin.
Don't worry about what shows from without but the love that lives within.
We're gonna get it all together, now, and everything gonna work out fine.
Just take a little time to look on the good side, my friend, and straighten it out in your mind.
(To Chorus:)

FROM A DISTANCE

Lyrics and Music by
JULIE GOLD

Slowly ♩ = 66

(with pedal)

%· Verse:

1. From a dis-tance, the world_ looks blue_
2.3. See additional lyrics

and green,_ and the snow-capped_ moun-tains, white.

From a

From a Distance - 5 - 1

© 1987 WING AND WHEEL MUSIC and JULIE GOLD MUSIC
Worldwide Rights for JULIE GOLD MUSIC Administered by CHERRY RIVER MUSIC CO.
All Rights for WING AND WHEEL MUSIC Administered by IRVING MUSIC, INC.
All Rights Reserved   Used by Permission

⊕ Coda

heart_____ of ev - 'ry___ man._____ It's the

hope of___ hopes,_ it's the love of___ loves.___ This is the song___ of___ ev - 'ry

Bridge:

man._____ And God_ is watch-ing us,___ God_ is watch-ing us,___ God_ is

watch-ing us_____ from a dis - tance._____ Oh, God is___ watch-ing us,___ God_ is

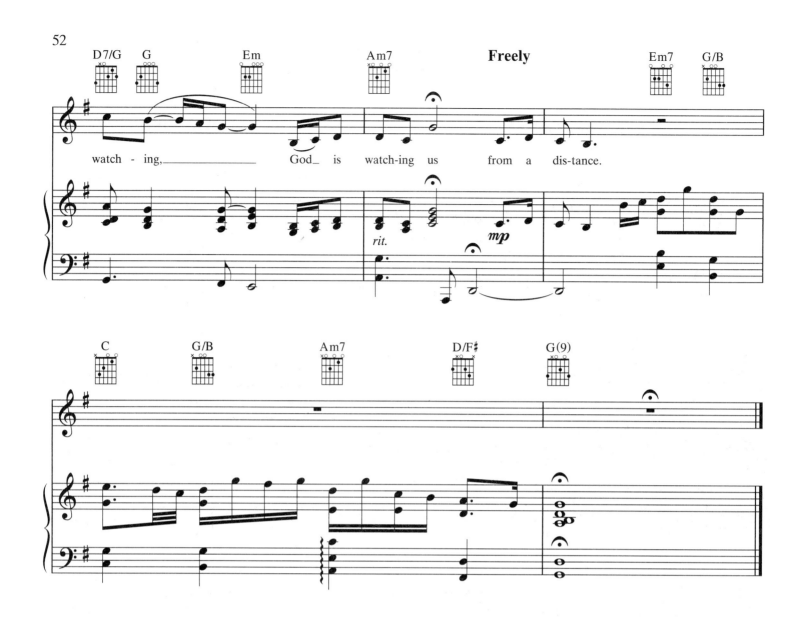

watch - ing,_____ God_ is watch-ing us from a dis-tance.

Freely

rit. *mp*

Verse 2:
From a distance, we all have enough,
And no one is in need.
There are no guns, no bombs, and no disease,
No hungry mouths to feed.

From a distance, we are instruments
Marching in a common band,
Playing songs of hope, playing songs of peace.
They're the songs of every man.

Verse 3:
From a distance, you look like my friend
Even though we are at war.
From a distance, I just cannot comprehend
What all this fighting is for.

From a distance, there is harmony,
And it echoes through the land.
It's the hope of hopes, it's the love of loves,
It's the heart of every man.
(To Bridge:)

HEART

Words and Music by
RICHARD ADLER and JERRY ROSS

Heart - 3 - 1

© 1955 FRANK MUSIC CORP.
Copyright Renewed and Assigned to LAKSHMI PUJA MUSIC LTD. and J & J ROSS MUSIC CO.
All Rights Administered by THE SONGWRITERS GUILD OF AMERICA
All Rights Reserved

HEAL THE WORLD

Written and Composed by
MICHAEL JACKSON
Prelude by
MARTY PAICH

There's a place.

in your heart___ and I know___ that it___ is love.___ And this place___
to know why___ there's a love___ that can-not lie.___ Love is strong,-
so___ high,.- let our spir - its nev - er die.___ In my heart,___

© 1991 MIJAC MUSIC (BMI)
All Rights Administered by WARNER-TAMERLANE PUBLISHING CORP. (BMI)
All Rights Reserved
PRELUDE: © 1991 HUDMAR PUBLISHING CO., INC. (ASCAP)
All Rights Reserved

GREATEST LOVE OF ALL

Words by
LINDA CREED

Music by
MICHAEL MASSER

Slowly ♩ = 66

(with pedal)

𝄋 *Verse:*

1.3. I be-lieve the chil-dren are our fu-ture; teach them well and let them lead the way.
be. 2. Ev-'ry-bod-y's search-ing for a he-ro; peo-ple need some-one to look up to.

Show them all the beau-ty they pos-sess in-side. Give them a
I nev-er found an-y-one who ful-filled my needs. A lone-ly

Greatest Love of All - 4 - 1

© 1977 (Renewed) EMI GOLD HORIZON MUSIC CORP. and EMI GOLDEN TORCH MUSIC CORP.
Exclusive Print Rights Administered by ALFRED MUSIC PUBLISHING CO., INC.
All Rights Reserved

64

HERO

Words and Music by
WALTER AFANASIEFF
and **MARIAH CAREY**

Hero - 6 - 1

© 1993 WB MUSIC CORP., WALLYWORLD MUSIC, SONGS OF UNIVERSAL, INC. and RYE SONGS
All Rights for WALLYWORLD MUSIC Administered by WB MUSIC CORP.
All Rights for RYE SONGS Administered by SONGS OF UNIVERSAL, INC.
All Rights Reserved

Bridge:

(YOUR LOVE KEEPS LIFTING ME) HIGHER AND HIGHER

Words and Music by
GARY JACKSON, CARL SMITH
and RAYNARD MINER

Fast ♩ = 190

(Your Love Keeps Lifting Me) Higher and Higher - 4 - 1

© 1967 (Renewed) UNICHAPPELL MUSIC INC., MIJAC MUSIC, WARNER-TAMERLANE PUBLISHING CORP. and CHEVIS MUSIC, INC.
All Rights on behalf of itself, MIJAC MUSIC and UNICHAPPELL MUSIC INC. Administered by WARNER-TAMERLANE PUBLISHING CORP.
All Rights Reserved

(Your Love Keeps Lifting Me) Higher and Higher - 4 - 4

I BELIEVE

Words and Music by
ERVIN DRAKE, IRVIN GRAHAM,
JIMMY SHIL and AL STILLMAN

Moderately, with much expression

I be-lieve for ev-'ry drop of rain that falls,_____ a flow-er

grows._____ I be-lieve that some-where in the

I Believe - 4 - 1

© 1952 (Renewed) LINDABET MUSIC, GENTLEMAN JIM MUSIC, J AND S FREEDOM MUSIC,
TRO-HAMPSHIRE HOUSE PUBLISHING, INC., TADZIO MUSIC COMPANY and LARRY SPIER MUSIC, LLC
All Rights for LINDABET MUSIC and GENTLEMAN JIM MUSIC Administered by The Songwriters Guild of America
All Rights Reserved

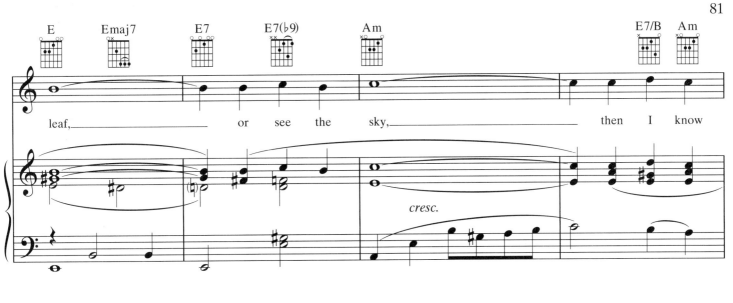

leaf,_____ or see the sky,_____ then I know

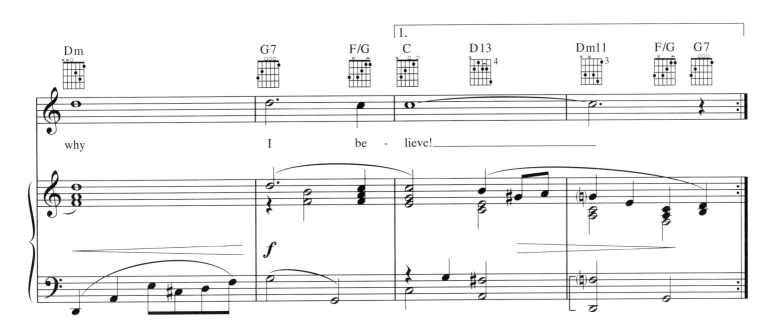

why   I   be - lieve!_____

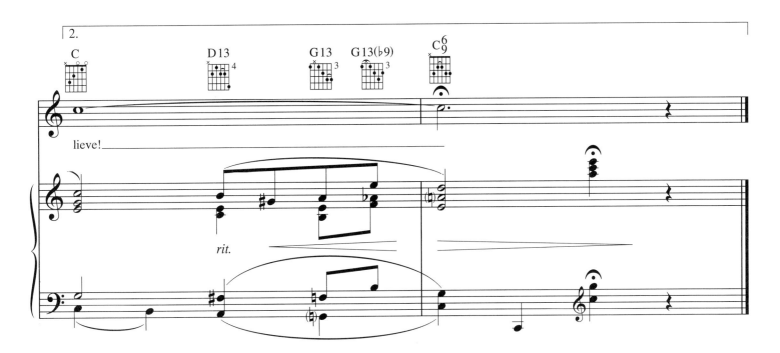

lieve!_____

I CAN SEE CLEARLY NOW

Words and Music by
JOHNNY NASH

Reggae ♩ = 120

Verse:

1. I can see clear - ly now,___ the rain___ is gone.___
2. Oh yes, I can make___ it now,___ the pain___ is gone.___
3. I can see clear - ly now,___ the rain___ is gone.___

I can see all___ ob - sta - cles___
All of the bad___ feel - ings have___
I can see all___ ob - sta - cles___

© 1972 (Renewed) NASHCO MUSIC
All Rights for the World Outside of North America Administered by WARNER/CHAPPELL MUSIC, LTD.
All Rights Reserved

Bridge:

Look all a - round,_____ there's noth - ing but blue skies._____

Look straight a - head, there's noth - ing but

blue skies._____

IN MY DAUGHTER'S EYES

Words and Music by
JAMES SLATER

© 2003 FSMGI (IMRO) and DIVERSION MUSIC (BMI)
All Rights Administered by STATE ONE MUSIC AMERICA (BMI)
All Rights Reserved

LIVE LIKE YOU WERE DYING

Words and Music by
TIM NICHOLS and
CRAIG WISEMAN

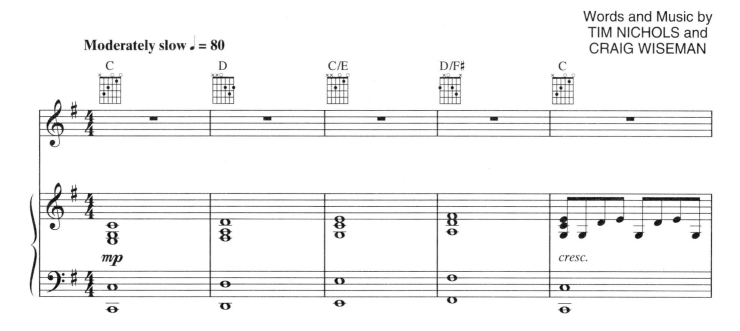

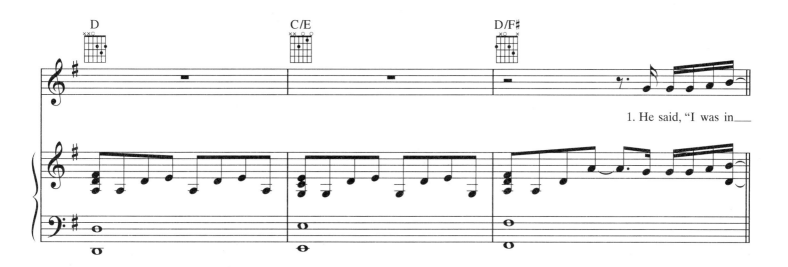

1. He said, "I was in____

____ my ear-ly for-ties with a lot of life___ be-fore___ me, when a
nal-ly___ the hus-band that most the time___ I was-n't, and I be-

© 2004 WARNER-TAMERLANE PUBLISHING CORP. and BIG LOUD SHIRT INDUSTRIES (Administered by BIG LOUD BUCKS, LLC) and BUG MUSIC
All Rights Reserved

"Some - day,___ I hope___ you___ get the chance to live___ like you were dy -

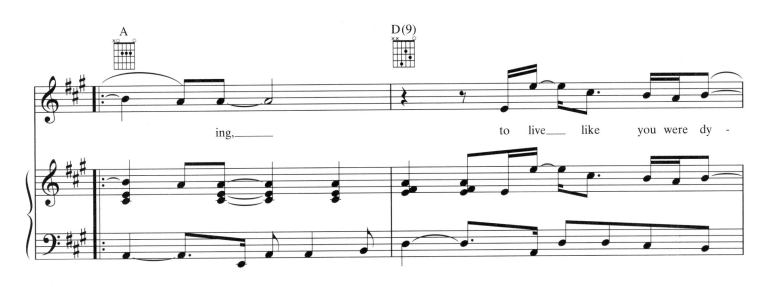

ing,_____ to live___ like you were dy -

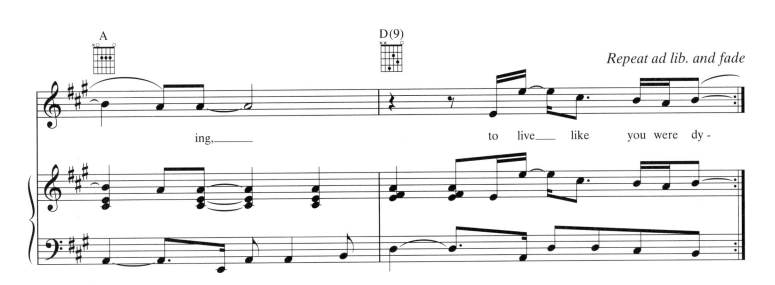

Repeat ad lib. and fade

ing,_____ to live___ like you were dy -

Live Like You Were Dying - 7 - 7

JUST A CLOSER WALK WITH THEE

TRADITIONAL

© 2010 ALFRED MUSIC PUBLISHING CO., INC.
All Rights Reserved

IT'S IN EVERY ONE OF US

Words and Music by
DAVID POMERANZ

It's in Every One of Us - 4 - 1

© 1973 (Renewed) WB MUSIC CORP. and UPWARD SPIRAL MUSIC
All Rights Administered by WB MUSIC CORP.
All Rights Reserved

LIFT EVERY VOICE AND SING

Words by
JAMES WELDON JOHNSON

Music by
JOHN ROSAMOND JOHNSON

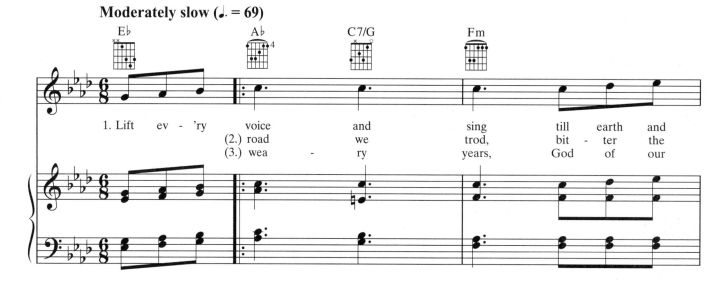

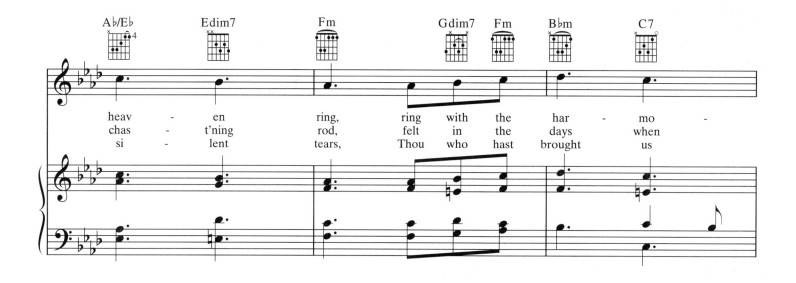

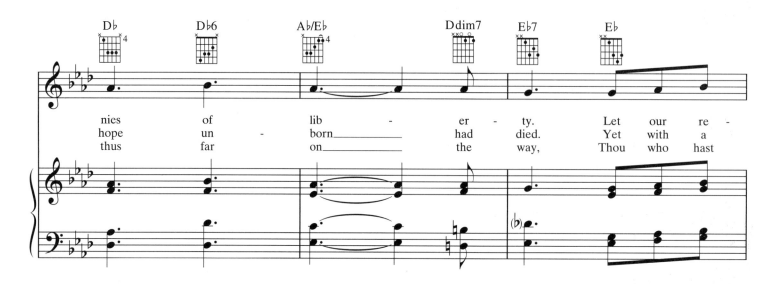

© 2010 ALFRED MUSIC PUBLISHING CO., INC.
All Rights Reserved

MAN IN THE MIRROR

Words and Music by
SIEDAH GARRETT and GLEN BALLARD

Medium

I'm gon-na make a change,___ for once in my_____ life.

It's gon-na feel___ real__ good,___ gon-na make a diff-erence, gon-na make it right.___

Man in the Mirror - 13 - 1

© 1987 Yellowbrick Road Music, Universal Music Corporation and Aerostation Corporation
All Rights for YELLOWBRICK ROAD MUSIC Administered by CHERRY LANE MUSIC PUBLISHING COMPANY
All Rights on behalf of itself and AEROSTATION CORPORATION Administered by UNIVERSAL MUSIC CORPORATION
Used by Permission of Cherry Lane Music Publishing Company
All Rights Reserved

116

Additional Lyrics for repeat:
(Yeah!-Make that change)
You know-I've got to get
 that man, that man...
(Man in the mirror)
You've got to
You've got to move! Come
 on! Come on!
You got to...
Stand up! Stand up!
 Stand up!
(Yeah!-Make that change)
Stand up and lift
 yourself, now!
(Man in the mirror)
Hoo! Hoo! Hoo!
Aaow!
(Yeah!-Make that change)
Gonna make that change...
 come on!
You know it!
You know it!
You know it!
You know...
(Change...)
Make that change.

THE MORNING AFTER

Words and Music by
AL KASHA and JOEL HIRSCHHORN

Verses 1 & 2:

1. There's got to be___ a morn - ing af - ter,
2. Oh, can't you see___ the morn - ing af - ter?

if we can hold___ on through___ the night.___
It's wait - ing right___ out - side_____ the storm.___

We have a chance___ to find___ the sun - shine,
Why don't we cross___ the bridge___ to - geth - er

The Morning After - 4 - 1

© 1972 (Renewed) WB MUSIC CORP. and WARNER-TAMERLANE PUBLISHING CORP.
All Rights Reserved

Repeat ad lib. and fade

LOOK TO THE RAINBOW

Words by
E.Y. HARBURG

Music by
BURTON LANE

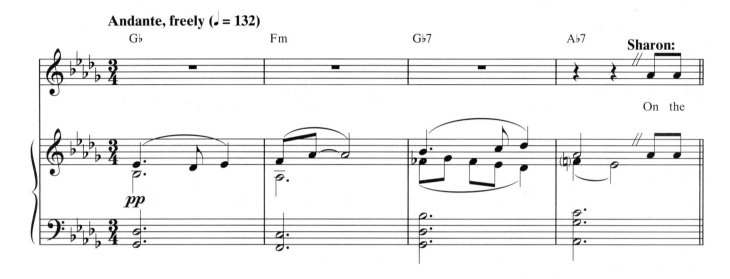

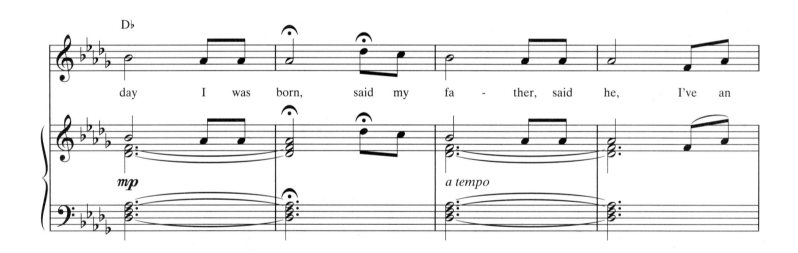

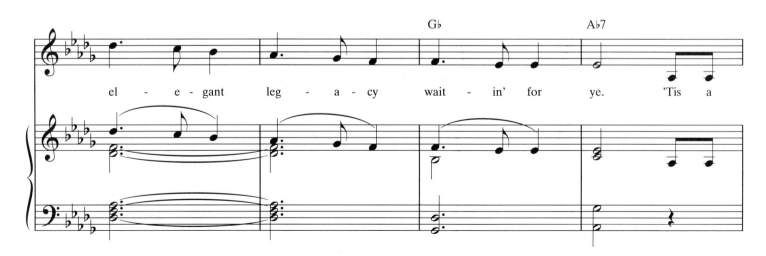

Look to the Rainbow - 5 - 1

© 1946 (Renewed) CHAPPELL & CO., INC. and GLOCCA MORRA MUSIC CORP.
(c/o NEXT DECADE ENTERTAINMENT, INC.)
All Rights Reserved

searched all the earth,__ and I scanned all the skies,__ but I

found it at last in my own true love's eyes.

Look, look, look to the rain - bow.

Fol - low it o - ver the hill___ and stream.

OH HAPPY DAY

Words and Music by
EDWIN R. HAWKINS

Oh Happy Day - 5 - 1

© 1969 KAMA-RIPPA MUSIC, INC. and EDWIN R. HAWKINS MUSIC CO.
All Rights Controlled by EMI U CATALOG INC. (Publishing) and ALFRED MUSIC PUBLISHING CO., INC. (Print)
All Rights Reserved

132

Bridge:

ONE MOMENT IN TIME

Words and Music by
ALBERT HAMMOND and JOHN BETTIS

Medium ballad

mp
smoothly

Verse 1:

1. Each day I live, I want to be a day to give the best of

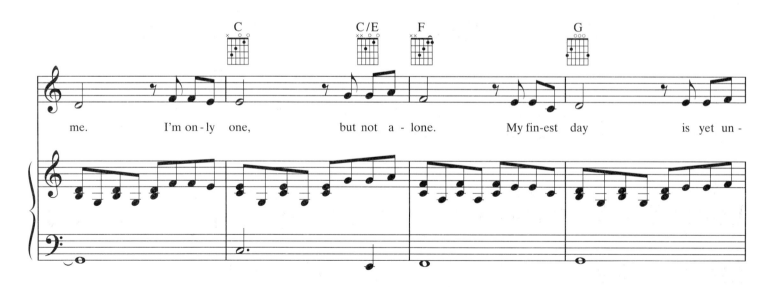

me. I'm on-ly one, but not a-lone. My fin-est day is yet un-

One Moment in Time - 5 - 1

© 1988 JOHN BETTIS MUSIC and ALBERT HAMMOND MUSIC
All Rights For JOHN BETTIS MUSIC Administered by WB MUSIC CORP.
All Rights Reserved

(THERE'LL BE) PEACE IN THE VALLEY

Words and Music by
THOMAS A. DORSEY

(There'll Be) Peace in the Valley - 3 - 1

© 1939 (Renewed) WARNER-TAMERLANE PUBLISHING CORP.
All Rights Reserved

THE PRAYER

Italian Lyric by
ALBERTO TESTA and TONY RENIS

Words and Music by
CAROLE BAYER SAGER and DAVID FOSTER

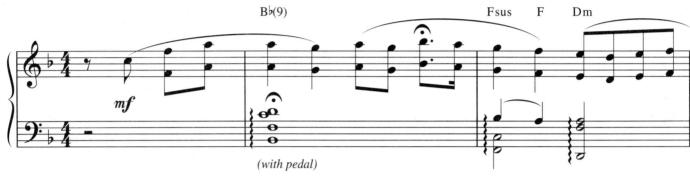

© 1996 WARNER-TAMERLANE PUBLISHING CORP. and WB MUSIC CORP.
All Rights Reserved

Verse 3:

SHOWER THE PEOPLE

Words and Music by
JAMES TAYLOR

Shower the People - 4 - 1

© 1975 (Renewed) COUNTRY ROAD MUSIC, INC.
All Rights Reserved

Vocal Ad Lib

They say in every life,
They say the rain must fall.
Just like a pouring rain,
Make it rain.
Love is sunshine.

SOFTLY AND TENDERLY

TRADITIONAL

Gently (♩. = 60)

Verse:

1. Soft - ly and ten - der - ly Je - sus is call - ing,
2. Why should we tar - ry when Je - sus is plead - ing,
3. Time is now fleet - ing, the mo - ments are pass - ing,
4. O for the won - der - ful love He has prom - ised,

call - ing for you and for me.
plead - ing for you and for me?
pass - ing from you and from me.
prom - ised for you and for me!

See, on the por - tals He's wait - ing and watch - ing,
Why should we lin - ger and heed not his mer - cies,
Shad - ows are gath - er - ing, death's night is com - ing,
Though we have sinned, He has mer - cy and par - don,

Softly and Tenderly - 2 - 1

© 2010 ALFRED MUSIC PUBLISHING CO., INC.
All Rights Reserved

TOUCH THE HEM OF HIS GARMENT

Words and Music by
SAM COOKE

Touch the Hem of His Garment - 3 - 1

© 1956 (Renewed) ABKCO MUSIC, INC., 85 Fifth Avenue, New York, NY 10003
All Rights Reserved

Verse 2:
Whoa, she spent her money here and there
Until she had no, had no more to spare.
The doctors they done all that they could
But their medicine would do no good.
When she touched Him, the Savior didn't see.
But still he turned around and cried,
"Somebody touched me."
She said, "It was I who just wanna touch the hem of your garment.
I know I'll be made whole right now."

Chorus 2:
She stood there crying, "Oh, Lord! Oh, Lord! Oh-oo-oh,
Oh, Lord! Oh, Lord!"
She said, "If I could just touch the hem of your garment,
I know I'll be made whole right now."

WHEN YOU BELIEVE

Music and Lyrics by
STEPHEN SCHWARTZ
with Additional Music by
BABYFACE

Slowly

(with pedal)

Verse:

1. Man - y nights we've prayed   with no proof an - y - one could hear,
2. In this time of fear,   when prayer so of - ten proved in vain,

in our hearts a hope - ful song we bare - ly un - der - stood. Now
hope seemed like the sum - mer birds, too swift - ly flown a - way. Yet

*Original recording a half step higher.

When You Believe - 7 - 1

© 1997 SKG SONGS (ASCAP)
Worldwide Rights for SKG SONGS Administered by CHERRY LANE MUSIC PUBLISHING COMPANY, INC.
All Rights Reserved   Used by Permission

When You Believe - 7 - 7

UP WHERE WE BELONG

Words by
WILL JENNINGS

Music by
JACK NITZSCHE and
BUFFY SAINTE-MARIE

Up Where We Belong - 4 - 1

© 1982 ENSIGN MUSIC CORP. and SONY/ATV HARMONY, 8 Music Square West, Nashville, TN 37203
All Rights Reserved

Chorus:

Love lift us up where we be-long,___ where the ea-gles cry___ on a

moun - tain high. Love lift us up where we be-long,___ far from the

Repeat ad lib. and fade

world we know;___ up where the clear winds___ blow.___

Verse 2:
Some hang on to "used-to-be,"
Live their lives looking behind.
All we have is here and now;
All our life, out there to find.
The road is long.
There are mountains in our way,
But we climb a step every day.
(To Chorus:)

WHAT A WONDERFUL WORLD

Words and Music by
GEORGE DAVID WEISS and BOB THIELE

What a Wonderful World - 4 - 1

© 1967 RANGE ROAD MUSIC INC. and QUARTET MUSIC INC.
Copyright Renewed 1995 by GEORGE DAVID WEISS and BOB THIELE
Rights for GEORGE DAVID WEISS Assigned to ABILENE MUSIC, INC. and Administered by LARRY SPIER MUSIC, INC.
All Rights Reserved

WHEN YOU'RE SMILING

Words and Music by
MARK FISHER, JOE GOODWIN
and LARRY SHAY

When You're Smiling - 4 - 1

© 1928 (Renewed) EMI MILLS MUSIC INC. and MUSIC BY SHAY (c/o The Songwriters Guild of America)
Exclusive Print Rights for EMI MILLS MUSIC INC. Administered by ALFRED MUSIC PUBLISHING CO., INC.
All Rights Reserved

WHO I WAS BORN TO BE

Words and Music by
AUDRA MAE BUTTS, JOHAN FRANSSON,
TOBIAS LUNDGREN and MIKAEL LARSSON

Who I Was Born to Be - 6 - 1

© 2009 WARNER/CHAPPELL MUSIC SCANDINAVIA AB, WB MUSIC CORP. and AMAEB
All Rights in the U.S. and Canada Administered by WB MUSIC CORP.
All Rights Reserved

180

Chorus:

Chorus:

THE WIND BENEATH MY WINGS

Words and Music by
LARRY HENLEY and JEFF SILBAR

Gently flowing, in 2 ♩ = 60

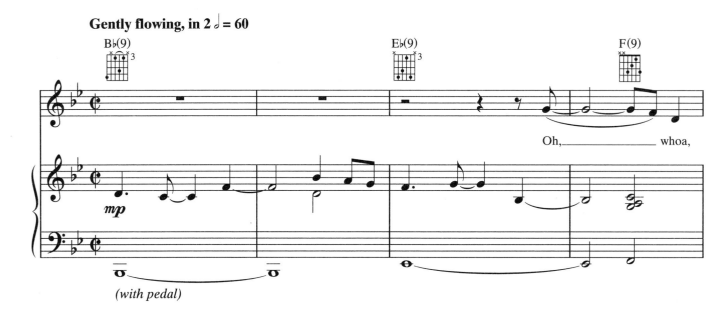

Oh,_____ whoa,

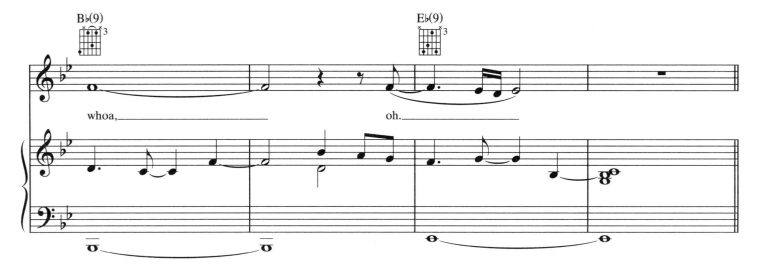

whoa,_____ oh.

Verse 1:

1. It must have been cold there in my shad-ow,____

The Wind Beneath My Wings - 7 - 1

© 1982 WARNER HOUSE OF MUSIC and WB GOLD MUSIC CORP.
All Rights Reserved

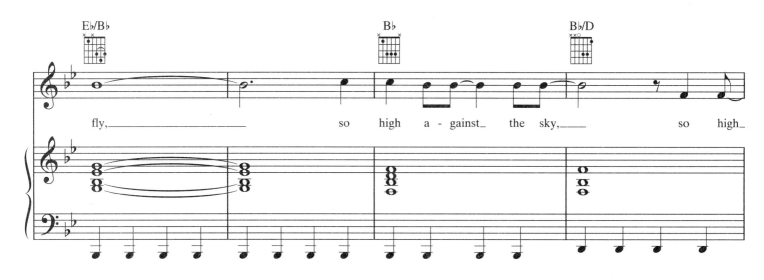

fly,_____ so high a - gainst_ the sky,____ so high_

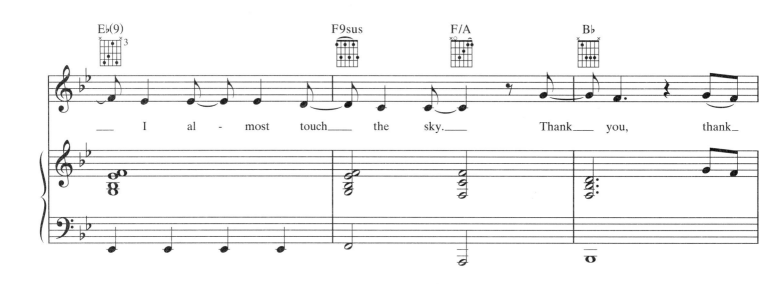

___ I al - most touch____ the sky.____ Thank____ you, thank_

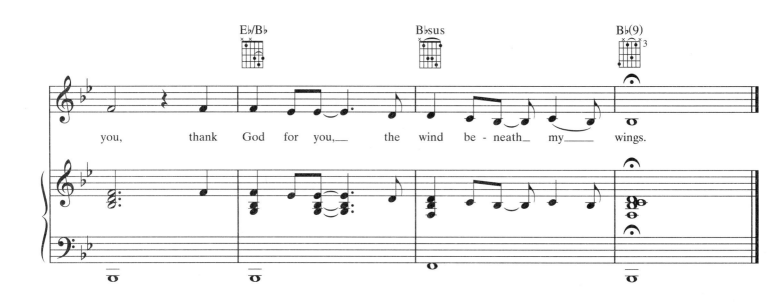

you, thank God for you,__ the wind be - neath_ my____ wings.

YOU LIGHT UP MY LIFE

Words and Music by
JOE BROOKS

You Light Up My Life - 3 - 1

© 1976 (Renewed) CURB SONGS (ASCAP) and UNIVERSAL–POLYGRAM INTERNATIONAL PUBLISHING, INC. (ASCAP)
All Rights Reserved

YOU RAISE ME UP

Words and Music by
ROLF LOVLAND and
BRENDAN GRAHAM

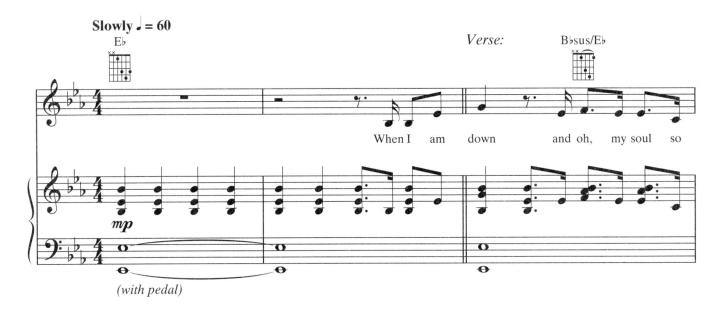

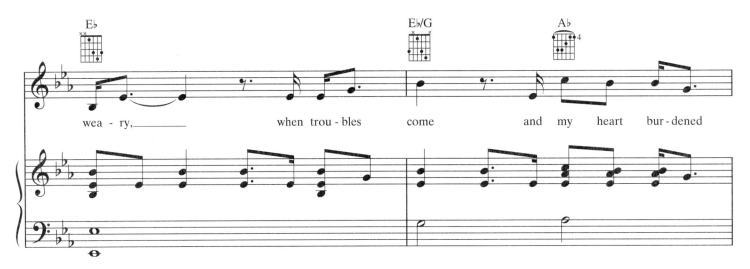

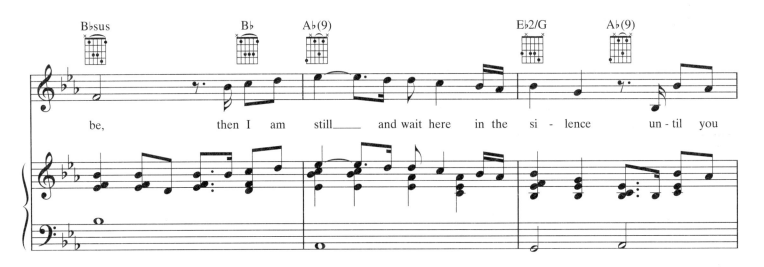

You Raise Me Up - 5 - 1

© 2002 UNIVERSAL MUSIC PUBLISHING, A Division of UNIVERSAL MUSIC AS and PEERMUSIC (Ireland) LTD.
All Rights for ROLF LOVLAND and UNIVERSAL MUSIC PUBLISHING Administered in the U.S. and Canada by
UNIVERSAL-POLYGRAM INTERNATIONAL PUBLISHING, INC. (Publishing) and ALFRED MUSIC PUBLISHING CO., INC. (Print)
All Rights Reserved

YOU'RE THE INSPIRATION

Words and Music by
DAVID FOSTER and PETER CETERA

© 1984 WARNER-TAMERLANE PUBLISHING CORP. and DOUBLE VIRGO MUSIC
All Rights Reserved

love some - bod - y; till the end — of time; when you
love some - bod - y; al - ways on — my mind. no one needs — you more than I. When you

Repeat ad lib. and fade

𝄋 *Verse 2:*
And I know (yes, I know)
That it's plain to see
We're so in love when we're together.
Now I know (now I know)
That I need you here with me
From tonight until the end of time.
You should know everywhere I go;
Always on my mind, you're in my heart, in my soul.

(To Chorus:)